Using Galaxy Tab

An Android Tablet

Marziah Karch

Apress®

Using Galaxy Tab: An Android Tab

ISBN-13 (pbk): 978-1-4842-0633-1

ISBN-13 (electronic): 978-1-4842-0632-4

Managing Director: Welmoed Spahr
Lead Editor: Steve Anglin
Development Editor: Matthew Moodie
Editorial Board: Steve Anglin, Gary Cornell, Louise Corrigan, James T. DeWolf,
    Jonathan Gennick, Robert Hutchinson, Michelle Lowman, James Markham,
    Matthew Moodie, Jeff Olson, Jeffrey Pepper, Douglas Pundick, Ben Renow-Clarke,
    Gwenan Spearing, Matt Wade, Steve Weiss
Coordinating Editor: Kevin Walter
Copy Editor: Laura Lawrie
Compositor: SPi Global
Indexer: SPi Global
Artist: SPi Global
Cover Designer: Anna Ishchenko

Distributed to the book trade worldwide by Springer Science+Business Media New York, 233 Spring Street, 6th Floor, New York, NY 10013. Phone 1-800-SPRINGER, fax (201) 348-4505, e-mail orders-ny@springer-sbm.com, or visit www.springeronline.com. Apress Media, LLC is a California LLC and the sole member (owner) is Springer Science + Business Media Finance Inc (SSBM Finance Inc). SSBM Finance Inc is a Delaware corporation.

For information on translations, please e-mail rights@apress.com, or visit www.apress.com.

Apress and friends of ED books may be purchased in bulk for academic, corporate, or promotional use. eBook versions and licenses are also available for most titles. For more information, reference our Special Bulk Sales–eBook Licensing web page at www.apress.com/bulk-sales.

Any source code or other supplementary material referenced by the author in this text is available to readers at www.apress.com/9781484208540. For detailed information about how to locate your book's source code, go to www.apress.com/source-code/.

This book would not exist without bagels.
Well, bread products in general.
Specifically, that blond guy in my kitchen baking them.
He's hot.

Contents at a Glance

Contents

About the Author

 **Marziah Karch** takes a special delight in the challenge of explaining new gadgets and complex technology to beginning audiences. She is the author of multiple books on technology topics. Marziah writes for About. com and GeekMom.com. Her articles have also appeared in Wired magazine.

Marziah was a senior educational technologist for Johnson County Community College in the Kansas City metro area for 14 years before she began working as a senior instructional designer for NWEA in Portland, Oregon. She holds a Master's in instructional design and is a doctoral student in Library and Information Management. When she's not feeding her geek side with new gadgets or writing about technology, Marziah enjoys keeping Portland weird with her husband and two children.

Acknowledgments

Thanks to Steve and the editorial staff at Apress for another fantastic job getting this book to press. I couldn't do it without such a great team.

I'd also like to thank my children, Pari and Kiyan. Without them, I would not have kids.

Introduction

Have you just purchased a Samsung Galaxy Tab S? If yes, let me tell you it was a fantastic choice. You'll love how light and responsive your tablet is, and you'll delight in all of the hidden features and bonus content. This book will have you up and running in no time.

If you're still on the fence and haven't purchased a tablet, this book can help with your decision.

Feel free to skim and skip around to find the sections that answer your biggest questions. There's no correct reading order. That said, if you haven't decided on a purchase, be sure to start with Chapter 1 for some juicy tips.

Chapter **1**

Getting Started

This chapter will guide you through all the typical steps you'll need to complete when you open up your shiny new Galaxy Tab. We'll also do a bit more than that. First we'll go over a few things to consider before you open that box. Is your tablet the right size? Will it work with your old apps? How well does it fit with other Samsung products? As always, if any of these sections don't quite apply to you (you already have a tablet, for example), then feel free to skip to the relevant parts.

Which Tablet Should You Buy?

There's obviously no single correct answer to this question, or else Samsung would only sell one tablet. The first and most obvious consideration is screen size. Screen size is measured diagonally, as shown in Figure 1-1.

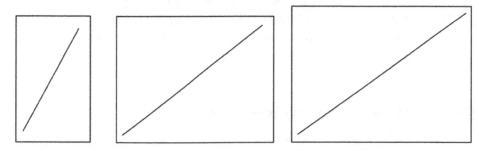

Figure 1-1. Screen sizes are measured diagonally in inches (left to right: 8.4, 10.5, and 12.2)

Currently the Samsung Tab S lineup consists of three basic sizes, 8.4, 10.5, and 12.2. The smaller the tablet, the smaller the price, with the smallest tablets in the S line currently retailing for around $380 and the largest weighing in at $550. Shop around, and there may be some bargains.

8.4 Tab S: This is a great size for someone who wants something light and easy to read while holding vertically in a single hand. The size is close to that of a paperback book. Samsung's small tablets are typically in this range between 7 and 8.5 inches. It weighs less than a pound, which makes it very easy to carry with you or hold in one unpropped hand. The smaller size makes for slightly less battery life, and it may not be a good choice if you like to watch movies or view books in larger print sizes.

10.5 Tab S: This is what many people would think of as "iPad sized," even though the iPad also comes in more than one size now. This is a great size for someone who wants to watch movies or read websites or maybe even occasionally use a Bluetooth keyboard. The weight is close to a pound and a half, which is still manageable for carrying around or holding with one hand, although not quite as comfortable.

12.2 Tab Pro: The much larger 12.2-inch "pro" tablet comes with twice the storage as a starter option (32 GB instead of 16 GB) and it is ideal for watching movies or surfing the web. Combined with a Bluetooth keyboard, this tablet can actually be used as a portable word processor or laptop alternative, although keep in mind that it does not run Windows software. It's also a bit bigger and heavier than the other tablets in the S series.

> **Note**   Microsoft makes a competing line of Surface tables that run a lightweight version of Windows 8 and can run Microsoft Office software. The operating system and battery life tend to suffer a little for trying to straddle the worlds of laptop users and tablet users, but it may be worth a look if you are a Windows user seeking a laptop replacement device.

Screen Resolution versus Screen Size

One important distinction here is screen resolution versus the screen size. The screens on these three tablets are obviously three very different sizes, but they all actually display the same amount of pixels: 2560x1600. Does that mean that the 12.2-inch Galaxy Pro looks worse than the 8.4-inch Galaxy Tab S? Actually, no. 2560 x 1600 is more resolution than an HDTV, which can be comfortably displayed on even a 100-inch screen. Effectively, a bigger screen means a bigger screen with a more pleasant viewing experience, and a smaller screen is just fine as long as you have good eyesight or hold it closer to your face.

Memory and Batteries

Memory and battery life are important considerations. Smaller tablets generally have a little less battery life because there's less tablet body in which to tuck away a larger battery, and less built-in hard drive space means less room to store apps, music, and movies. Both the 8.4- and 10.5-inch Galaxy Tab S models start at 16 GB of memory, while the Galaxy Tab Pro starts at 32 GB. You can purchase a Galaxy Tab S with 32 GB of memory for around $50 more. It may be a wise investment. Space runs out pretty quickly. All three Galaxy S Tab models have the same processor speed.

Used and Refurbished

Samsung occasionally sells refurbished Galaxy Tabs at a discount. They've been offered on Woot.com, Amazon Warehouse, Overstock.com, Cowboom. com, and other websites. It may be worth a look. Although "refurbished" can mean that the item was broken, often it just means someone purchased it and then returned it, so it can no longer be sold as a "new" item.

What Is Android?

Back in 2005, two years before Apple would revolutionize the phone world with the iPhone, Google bought a small, two-year-old company founded by Andy Rubin. Rubin was best known at the time for starting Danger, Inc., which created the T-Mobile–branded Sidekick phones. Rubin's new company, Android, also included Richard Minor from Orange (a U.K. phone company), Chris White from WebTV, and Andy McFadden from WebTV and Moxi. Originally, Rubin approached Google for possible startup money, but Google ended up acquiring Android and the talented team behind it.

What was so different about Android? Previous phone operating systems were either made by the device manufacturer or licensed to them for a fee. Rubin's idea was to give away the operating system and find some other way to make money. Because Google gives away most of their Web products for free and makes money from advertising, the idea resonated with Google.

On November 5, 2007, Google announced the Android OS and the Open Handset Alliance, a group of companies that would help develop it. Open Handset Alliance members include phone carriers, software developers, device manufacturers, and component makers.

Android had a very different philosophy when compared to Apple and the iPhone. Anyone could use Android in devices for free, anyone could modify Android, and anyone could develop apps for it without seeking permission to put their apps in the Android Market.

Google also seeded the Android app market by holding developer contests with cash prizes, so by the time the first Android phone arrived in stores, there was a selection of apps available for download.

Today, Android has moved beyond the phone. It's powering eBook readers, tablets, photo frames, Google TV, netbooks, and even car stereos.

Samsung's Ecosystem

Samsung really does have its own galaxy. Although Google makes Android, most manufactures put their own little spin on the operating system. What Samsung offers Is mostly the same as other Android devices, but there are interface changes Samsung makes to its product line to add features. The Android version shipping with the Galaxy Tab is "Kit Kat," and the specific interface changes Samsung makes are called "Touchwiz."

Samsung makes a lot of different Android-powered devices, including the Galaxy S phone line, the Galaxy Note phone line, Android watches, and the Galaxy Tab and Tab S series. All of these devices are compatible with each other and may offer NFC beaming between devices or easy Bluetooth syncing. However, in most cases, you don't need to have an all-Samsung device lineup in order to use your phone and your tablet together. You do have to have a Samsung tablet or phone to use it with some of the Samsung watches, and you need a Samsung TV to use your tablet as a remote control.

Setting Up Your Galaxy Tab

Once you decide a Galaxy Tab is the tablet for you, you can open the box, plug in the charging cable, and then get started with the initial setup, as shown in Figure 1-2.

Figure 1-2. Choose a language

Accessibility Options

If you choose the "Accessibility" option as shown in Figure 1-2, you'll have the opportunity to change settings immediately before setup. You're not locked out of the Accessibility menu forever if you want to change the settings later. You can also create an accessibility shortcut toggle in order to rapidly change settings if you share a device. We'll cover sharing devices and parental settings in Chapter 5.

Accessibility options for Galaxy Tab include three basic areas, Vision, Hearing, and Dexterity.

Vision options include:

■ Dark Screen—make the screen dark all the time. Why would you want to do this? If you are vision-impaired to the point that you cannot see the screen, keeping it dark keeps people from looking over your shoulder. It also saves battery life.

■ Rapid Key Input—you can either double tap (the default) or click once and release in order to make a selection.

■ Speak passwords—rather than typing them, you can use voice recognition to enter your password.

- Text to speech—This feature uses a computer voice to read back any text and selections.

- Large fonts—you can change the system fonts to make them larger and easier to see or change the contrast. You can also set specific magnification gestures to increase the size of the screen and zoom in on particular areas, even when you are not using an app with a zoom feature.

Hearing accessibility options include the option to turn sound off completely (so as not to annoy anyone when the tablet makes noise you can't hear) and turn on flash notifications (rather than sound). You can also turn subtitles on in Google and Samsung videos by default (when subtitles are offered).

Dexterity options include the ability to make an "Assistant menu" with quick functions, adding a press and hold delay for selections, and the ability to block or unblock areas of the screen from interacting to touch.

Date and Time

Once you start your device, you need to set up the date and time. Figure 1-3 shows the very first screen. This is fairly straightforward. Don't rush this and skip through without setting the date, however. Sometimes an incorrect date and time setting can cause syncing errors with Android tablets.

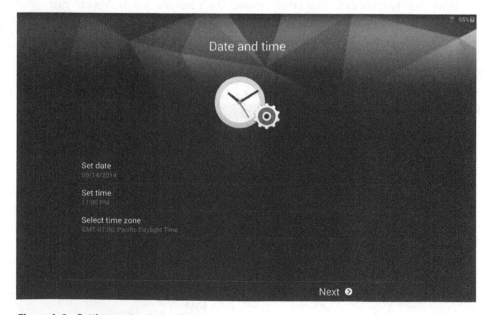

Figure 1-3. Setting up the date and time

EULA

You'll be asked to agree to the EULA (end user license agreement) in order to continue (Figure 1-4). You'll also be asked about using data from your tablet to help Samsung develop future updates or tablets. Samsung states that the data will be used in the aggregate and deleted after seven months. Whether or not you agree to this use is up to you. It won't impact your current ability to use your tablet. Note that you will have to turn it on if you want the keyboard prediction to remember personalized data.

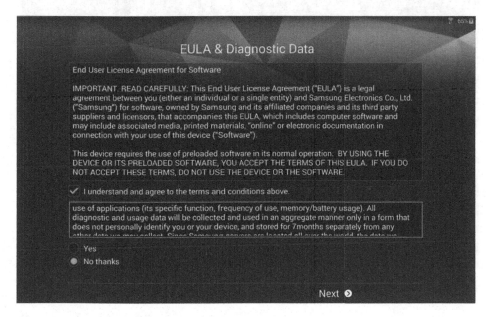

Figure 1-4. The EULA and big data agreements

Note   Big data is a method of gathering as much aggregate, anonymous data as possible about as many users as possible and then analyzing it for patterns. Amazon uses big data to make recommendations about purchases (people who like X product also consider Y product) and apps such as Google Maps use big data to find out about traffic jams and average commute times. Samsung uses big data to figure out predictive text on the keyboard, among other things.

Wi-Fi

If you're opening your tablet in an area with an open wireless account (something I do not recommend doing, because you have to input passwords, and those could be intercepted over unencrypted wireless networks), you will not need to set up Wi-Fi. Everyone else will see a screen like that shown in Figure 1-5.

Figure 1-5. Time to set up the wireless

Setting up your wireless account is fairly straightforward. Select your wireless network from the list of available networks by tapping on it, and then enter the password (Figure 1-6). A keyboard will automatically appear when text entry is required. There are advanced options available if you need them, but for most home networks this is sufficient.

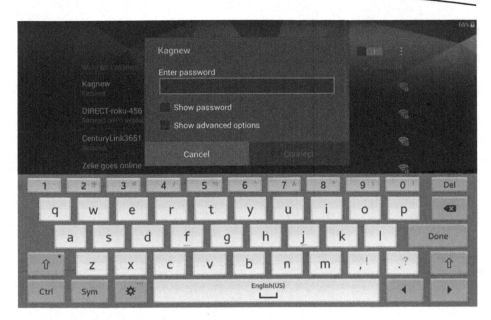

Figure 1-6. Set up the wireless network

Google Account

If you don't have a Google Account (usually your Gmail address), you can set one up at this time. You need to have a Google account in order to download Google Play apps, receive Gmail messages, or use Google's backup features for Android tablets.

If you have an existing Google account, no worries. Enter it now, and you'll start downloading preferences and other settings from your previous Google account. If you are using two-step verification (Figure 1-7), you will have to enter the verification code texted to your phone in order to set up a new device.

Figure 1-7. Two-step verification

> **Tip** Two-step verification is a way to prevent having your Google account hacked. This is an opt-in service that you can set up through Google, which will require you to get a text message on your phone every time you set up a new Google account anywhere.

Google Services

You can now choose which Google services you'd like to enable, such as data backup and location tracking (Figure 1-8). **Backup and Restore** will help you recover information from your tablet if it crashes and needs to be reset, but it will also allow you to download data from backups made on previous tablets or phones using Android. More options are available if you keep scrolling by tapping the down arrow or using your finger in a swiping motion to scroll.

Figure 1-8. Google permissions

You'll also be prompted to set up Google Photos if you have a Google+ account (Figure 1-9). If you used previous versions of Android, there was an app called Gallery that stored photos and allowed you to share. In this version of android (KitKat), the app is called Photos and allows photos to be synced with Google+ and enhanced with Auto Awesome to either add automatic digital effects or create virtual scrapbooks called "moments."

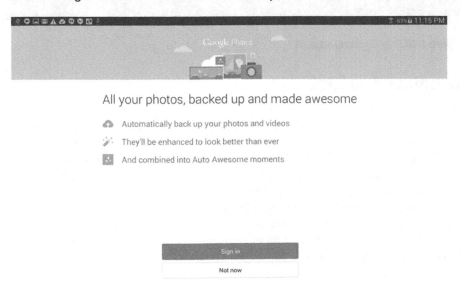

Figure 1-9. Permission to sync the Photo app

Samsung Account

Now you can set up your Samsung account (Figure 1-10). Yes, you've set up your Google account, but Samsung also maintains a separate app store. Registration is free, and Samsung provides some free app goodies for anyone who signs in with their account or registers a new account. Samsung also sent me a coupon for a half-price accessory when I registered the tablet, but that may be a limited time offer.

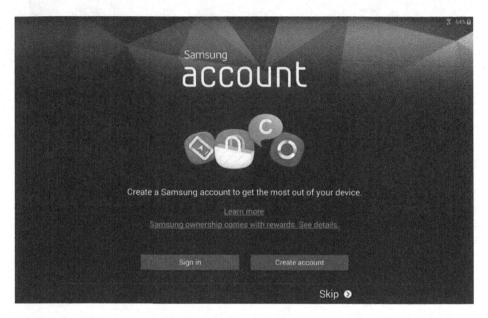

Figure 1-10. The Samsung account

Dropbox Account

Do you have a Dropbox account? If so, you can enter your account information now. Otherwise, you can create a new Dropbox account. As a perk of buying a Samsung Galaxy Tab S series tablet, you get 50 TB of online storage for two years (Figure 1-11). You don't have to take the storage space if you don't want it, but it does come in very handy. For example, you can store backup copies of documents and photos. It makes it easy to edit documents on your desktop computer and then view or edit them on your tablet. I scan a copy of my children's school documents to have on hand on my phone during parent-teacher conferences, and I save backups of my books and academic papers as I write them.

Figure 1-11. Sign up for a Dropbox account

Local TV Information

Your Galaxy Tab acts like a remote control for Samsung TVs. If you don't own a Samsung TV, you can still use your Galaxy Tab as a virtual TV guide to tell you what is on TV at any given moment. If you're interested in using this feature, go ahead and set it up, as shown in Figure 1-12.

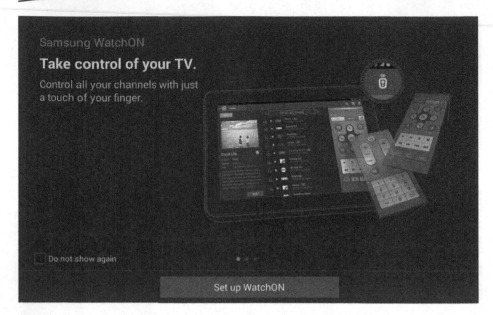

Figure 1-12. Set up WatchON by entering your local cable or terrestrial signal information

Device Name

The final step in the initial setup process is to input your name for personalization (Figure 1-13) and then enter a device name in order to enable sharing over local networks and by Bluetooth. You can accept the default name or customize it to something unique. This is a public name that will be visible on your local intranet, so it's a good idea to keep the name G-rated (Figure 1-14).

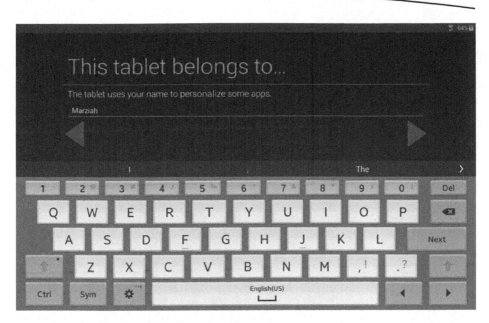

Figure 1-13. *Enter your name for personalization*

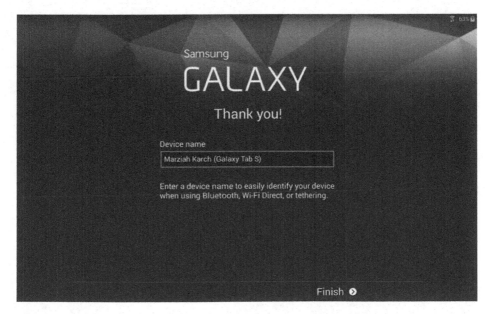

Figure 1-14. *Enter a unique device name that you'll recognize on the network*

Figure 1-14 shows you that you're finally done with the initial setup. Tap Finish, and you're done.

That's it. Now that your Galaxy Tab is set up and syncing with the network, you can take a break and allow everything to sync. In the next chapter, we'll explore the Samsung Galaxy Tab interface in more detail and add your non-Gmail email accounts.

Chapter 2

Navigating the Galaxy Tab

In the last chapter, we went through the initial setup for your new Galaxy Tab. Now it is time to explore the interface and features of your new Galaxy Tab.

The Physical Buttons and Hardware

Figure 2-1 shows the hardware features visible on the front and sides of the 10.2 inch Galaxy S tablet.

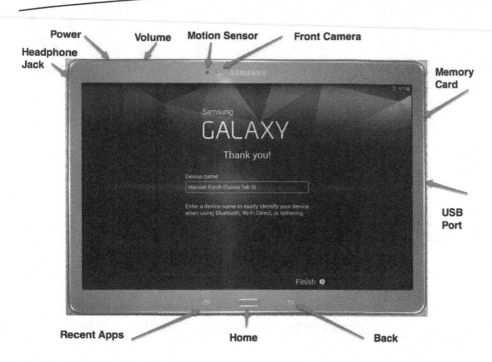

Figure 2-1. The front of the 10.2 inch tablet

On the top of the tablet, you can see what looks like two cameras. Instead, it's actually one camera and a motion/proximity sensor. The motion sensor is used for gesture control. For example, the screen capture gesture is swiping your hand from the right to the left of the screen.

The top edge of the tablet has two buttons. The short button is the power button, and the longer button is the volume toggle.

The bottom of the tablet has three buttons. This is mostly familiar to Samsung phone owners. The Back button to the right goes either back to the previous screen or closes an open app, depending on where you are in the app. The Home button returns you to the Home screen (we'll describe what that is as we progress through this chapter). The Recent Apps button is in the place where most Samsung phones put the Menu button. Recent Apps lets you toggle between recently opened apps. This is actually a pretty standard configuration for Android tablets, although the Nexus series tablets from Google swap the position of the Back and Recent Apps button.

Rounding out the physical hardware are the jacks and ports. There's a headphone jack, a USB Port, and an SD card slot. On the back of the tablet, there is a rear-facing camera with flash and an infrared blaster for using as a remote control with Samsung TVs.

TouchWiz UI

As mentioned in Chapter 1, Samsung created a modified version of Android with the TouchWiz UI (User interface). TouchWiz adds a few features to your tablet, and Samsung provides a few new apps that take advantage of this new interface.

Home Screen

The Home Screen is not the first thing that you see when you turn your device on. It is usually the second. The first thing you see is the Lock Screen, which we will get to later in this chapter. If you swipe to open your device (the default setting), you'll see the Home Screen. Figure 2-2 shows a fresh Galaxy Tab S Home screen with all of the basic interface parts labeled.

Figure 2-2. The Home Screen

Let's go over each part and the role that they play in using your Galaxy Tab.

Notification Icons

Notification icons are little alerts to let you know that something has happened in the background, such as you have a new email message, one of your apps was updated, your download has finished, your friend has made a new Facebook post, or you were just mentioned in a tweet. App programmers can create custom icons and choose when apps give you a notification, if at all.

If you see notifications and want to see more details, just drag your finger from the top of the screen downward, as if you're pulling shade down on a window. You'll see a screen similar to Figure 2-3. This is the notification panel.

Figure 2-3. The Notification Panel

The notification panel is a one-stop action shop for your notifications, but it also lets you quickly change preferences. This is a TouchWiz enhancement, as the standard Android tablet just pulls down a simple notification panel. We'll circle back to this screen for more details, but right now let's focus on the notifications.

The small notifications on the top of the screen are now larger icons with more information, and you can take some actions, depending on the notification. If you have an email message, you can tap on it to open the message. Tap on a downloaded or updated app to launch it. Photos offer the option to either launch photo editing or share.

If you don't want to see a notification anymore (an email message you'll ignore until later, for example) swipe the notification to the left with your finger to dismiss it.

Status Icons

Status icons let you know about your device, including your battery charge level, the clock's time, the tablet's Wi-Fi status, GPS status, and speaker status (on or muted to vibrate only).

Widgets

Widgets are small, often interactive apps that run on a portion of your Home screen. There are widgets that display weather information, allow you to control your playlists, display your eBook library, and more. By default, the first widgets you'll see will be links to download free Samsung apps and bonus content. By tapping on the widget, you'll launch the Samsung app store to download the free bonus apps (Figure 2-4). This requires that you have a Samsung account, as covered in Chapter 1.

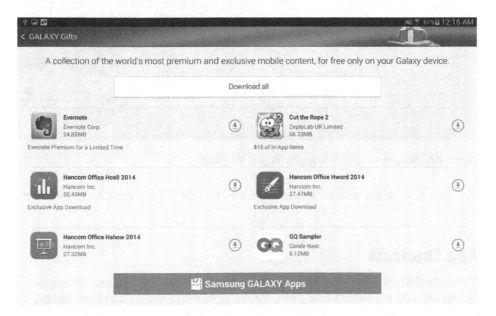

Figure 2-4. The Samsung bonus apps

Once you've installed your bonus apps, there's no point in keeping the widget on your Home screen. It's easy to remove it:

1. Press your finger down on the widget and hold it until you feel the tablet vibrate slightly (this is known as the long-press).

2. Keep your finger pressed to the widget and drag it upward onto the trash icon labeled "Remove" (Figure 2-5).

Figure 2-5. Remove widgets by dragging them to the trash

You can also resize and reposition widgets by using the long-press and then dragging.

App Shortcuts

These small icons on your Home screen are just shortcuts to launch apps. Using the same method you'd use for widgets (long-press and then drag), you can remove app shortcuts from your Home screen or drag them to different positions.

Note   Removing an app from the Home screen does not delete the app. It just removes the Home screen shortcut.

My Files

Tap on this shortcut to see all of the files on your tablet. If you've ever used an older Android tablet, you'll really appreciate how amazing it is to see all your files. This includes documents, music, pictures, and even apps. Figure 2-6 shows the My Files area. (In my case, My Files was full of screen captures used to write this book.)

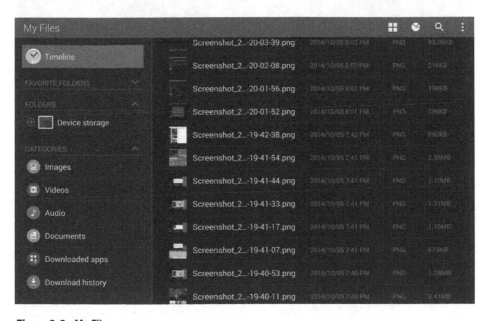

Figure 2-6. My Files

Home Screen Navigation

The Home screen on the Galaxy Tab S is a bit different than a standard Android tablet. The Galaxy S offers two main home screens, which you can use for app shortcuts or widgets. Swipe left or right to switch between screens.

There's also a third (and fourth) screen that provide a tiled view. Swipe three times to get to this view or just tap on the tiled icon in the Home screen navigation area. Think of this as widgets on steroids. Figure 2-7 shows the default configuration for the first tiled Home screen view.

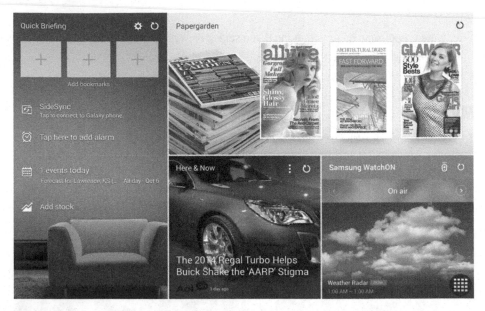

Figure 2-7. Tiled view of the Home screen

The second screen (Figure 2-8) default is all about office productivity and offers email, calendar, and document editing widgets.

Figure 2-8. The second tiled Home screen view centers on productivity

You can add or remove tiled widgets from these two screens by long-press dragging, just as you can with the default Home screen view, as shown in Figure 2-9.

Figure 2-9. Editing the default layout

Apps

In the earliest versions of Android, the app tray was invoked from the bottom of the screen like a tool drawer. In the Galaxy Tab S, the app area is just launched by tapping on the icon on the bottom right corner of the screen (Figure 2-10). Here the screens can be navigated by swiping left or right with a finger, and you will go through as many screens as it takes to display all the apps and only apps in this area. Other versions of Android put widgets in this area as well, but Samsung puts them in a separate area.

Figure 2-10. The Apps screen

Going Beyond the Home Screen Basics

Now that we've explored the basic interface, let's circle back and dig a little deeper with a few of those screens. First, let's revisit the Notification Panel and get to know it a little better.

The Notification Panel

As you saw earlier, swipe with your finger downward from the top of the screen to invoke the Notification Panel. Let's take a look at the top area first, as shown in Figure 2-11.

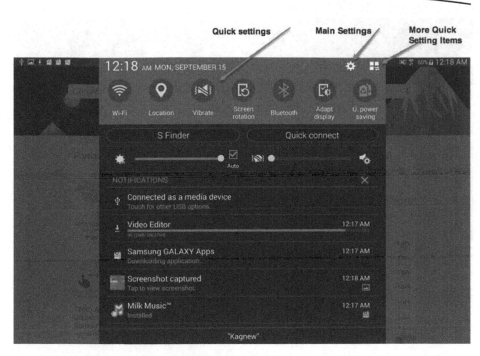

Figure 2-11. The top row of the Notification Panel

There are a lot of hidden features here. First, we have the quick settings. If you want to toggle your Wi-Fi on or off, set the sound to vibrate only, or turn on Bluetooth, you can do that with a single tap. If you need to adjust the main settings or preferences, you can do so by tapping the gear shape. You would use the gear shape for doing something more complex, such as adding an email account or changing your location settings for the internal clock.

The square window-looking icon is actually a link to even more quick settings, as shown in Figure 2-12.

Figure 2-12. All the quick settings

You probably aren't going to use all of those settings often, and you may not use some of the default quick settings that often, either. Adjust which quick settings appear in your Notification Panel by tapping on the pencil icon on the top of this screen.

Now we'll move on to the items just under the quick settings (Figure 2-13). Here you'll see the S Finder and Quick Connect.

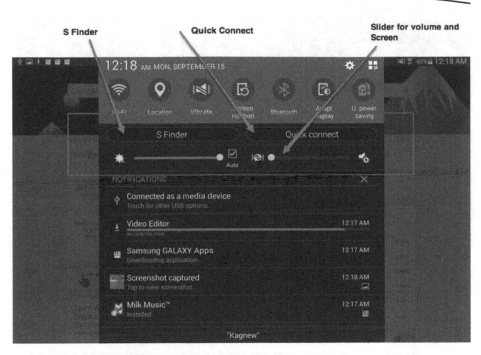

Figure 2-13. The Quick connect and S Finder

These two buttons are used in conjunction with other devices. S Finder finds other Samsung devices, such as TVs and phones, so you can quickly share content, for example, sharing a song or a video file. The Quick Connect is similarly meant for quick file sharing, only centered on non-Samsung devices, such as laptop computers.

Below the buttons, you'll see slider controls for screen brightness and volume. The Quick Settings button can toggle volume on or off, but this lets you fine-tune it.

Deeper into My Files

The second area to explore further is the My Files screen, which you launch by tapping on the My Files icon from the bottom left of the Home screen.

The first area to notice is on the left side of the screen, as shown in Figure 2-14.

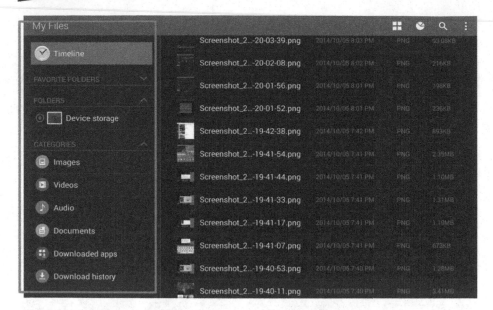

Figure 2-14. The filters for My Files

If you want to know what you have on your device, sometimes it's helpful to not have it all in a jumble. You can sort by when an item was downloaded by tapping on the Timeline button. Sort by items that are stored on your SD card (if you have one installed) by tapping on Device storage. Filter items to only images, videos, documents, apps, or audio files by tapping on the respective filter. You can also swipe upward to find more filtering choices, including the ability to filter items to only those stored in Dropbox.

The next area to notice is the upper right corner (Figure 2-15).

Figure 2-15. View options

The first icon looks like a series of squares. If you tap on this, it will change the My Files display from the default list view to large icons. Tap it again for smaller icons, and tap it a third time to return to list view. The pie chart shows the tablet's data usage. This is important if you have a tablet with a built in cellular data plan. Because downloads eat up a lot of data, you can check usage from this view. The magnifying glass Is Search, of course. In this case, you can search through your files by name. The final icon offers more "menu" choices. You can sort the files, for example.

The final thing to pay attention to is the information on the items themselves. In list view, you can see the file name, size, type, and date the file was last modified. This is pretty powerful stuff.

Summary

In this chapter, we learned more abut the interface in the Galaxy Tab S. It uses a modified version of Android called TouchWiz and offers more features than the standard Android tablet. In the next chapter, we'll explore some practical ways to use your Galaxy Tab S.

Chapter 3

Freebies and Bonus Content

In the last chapter, we explored the Galaxy Tab interface and a few of the unusual quirks. In this chapter we'll continue setting up our Samsung Galaxy Tab with all the free and discounted items that were included with the purchase. Some of these items are limited time offers, so they may not be available when you read this book. However, Samsung often makes new apps to make devices compatible with each other. Keep checking the Samsung store to find more. One of the advantages of buying a Samsung tablet over a cheaper generic Android tablet Is that Samsung has provided a bunch of goodies for new owners.

> **Note** Some of these promotions, such as the free Hunger Games movie, will expire after a certain number of downloads and are only available for a limited amount of time. Take all of the promotions that are available to you, and download all of the free apps. You can delete the apps you don't want from your device and still have access to them later if you change your mind.

You'll find some of your bonus content by tapping on the Galaxy Essentials/Galaxy Gifts widget, which appears by default on your Home Screen (Figure 3-1).

Figure 3-1. The Galaxy Essentials and Galaxy Gifts widget

You also had the chance to unlock a gift when you registered your Galaxy Tab (as shown in Chapter 1). Samsung offered a free Dropbox account with extra storage space, and (at least at the time of my registration) you had the chance to purchase a Galaxy Tab accessory at a discount.

Galaxy Essentials

The Galaxy Essentials apps are Samsung-exclusive apps that will only work on your Samsung device and are downloaded from the Samsung app store. Some of the apps are also only useful in conjunction with another Samsung device. Tap on the Galaxy Essentials widget on the Home screen to be taken to the store (see Figure 3-2).

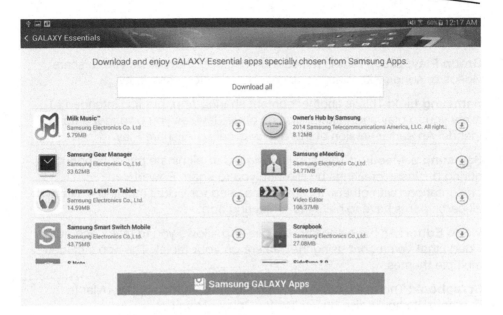

Figure 3-2. The Samsung Essentials

The apps include:

Milk Music: This is a streaming "radio station" app powered by Slacker Radio.

Samsung Gear: This app is useful if you have Samsung gear, including Samsung smart watches. You can use the app to pair devices and install apps on them. If you have an Android Wear watch by someone other than Samsung, use the Android Wear app.

Samsung Level: This app is intended to support the sound system for connected Samsung Bluetooth headphones or speakers.

Samsung Smart Switch Mobile: This app helps you upgrade and migrate from a previous device, such as an iPhone or an older non-Samsung Android device.

Samsung Note: This is a note-taking app that you can either sync with Evernote or with your Samsung account. If you have a Galaxy Note phone, this should be very familiar.

Owner's Hub: This app integrates with your Samsung account and is essentially an advertising vehicle for Samsung promotions. Provide your demographic information and preferences, and it offers promotions. It also offers a lot of coupons and freebies for tablet owners.

S Translator: This is a translation app that offers support for 11 languages, and it offers the ability to translate spoken words into another language.

Group Play: Group Play is a media sharing app that allows you to share videos or songs with other Samsung users in close proximity.

Samsung Link: This is another content sharing app, but it is intended to allow you to play and transfer files on other devices you own, not among friends. An earlier version of this app was called Allshare Play.

Samsung e-Meeting: This app is designed to eliminate paper handouts during business meetings by allowing you to share PowerPoint presentations with others. It can also be used for virtual meetings, although all participants have to have the e-Meeting app.

Video Editor: As the name implies, this app allows you to make and edit videos that you record using the camera on your tablet. The app includes multiple themes.

Scrapbook: This is a picture-collecting and annotation app, similar to Evernote. It should also be familiar for Galaxy Note users.

SideSync: SideSync is a screensharing app to share your screen on Galaxy phones or computers.

Story Album: Story Album is a virtual photo scrapbooking app. Photos you compile here can also be printed out as physical book, so it's an option for vacation photos.

Smart Tutor: This is a remote support app for diagnosing problems and/or asking quick support questions.

Galaxy Gifts

Galaxy Gifts are apps that are available for other devices but are offered to Samsung users as promotional gifts. Not all apps may be available as you read this, as there is a limited time span on some of these offers.

Evernote: This is a fantastic note-taking and web-clipping app. Samsung is offering a year of Evernote Premium service for a limited time.

Cut the Rope 2: This is a puzzle game in which you figure out how and when to cut rope in order to feed a critter a piece of candy. It's actually pretty fun. The offer is for $15 of in-app purchases.

Hancom Office Hcell 2014: This is a premium Excel equivalent spreadsheet program.

Hancom Office Hword 2014: This is a premium Microsoft Word compatible word processor for tablets.

Hancom Office Hshow 2014: This rounds out the Office-equivalent suite with slide presentations compatible with PowerPoint.

Stitcher Radio for Podcasts: This app allows you to assemble a series (stich) of podcasts.

Box: Box is a cloud-storage app similar to Dropbox, and the offer is for 50 GB of storage for six months.

Marvel Unlimited: This is a comic book app for Marvel fans, and the offer is for a three-month trial.

The Economist: This is a six-month virtual newspaper subscription.

The Wall Street Journal: This is a six-month trial subscription to the famous business newspaper.

Play Newsstand: This is a six-month subscription to a "Best of" app for various popular Conde Nast magazines. Samplers available include:

- Vanity Fair
- Self
- Vogue
- Wired
- Architectural Digest
- Glamour
- Lucky
- GQ

Workout Trainer: Workout Trainer is a virtual exercise training app that offers variable workouts with video tutorials. Samsung offers a six-month "pro" subscription.

Family Guy: The Quest for Stuff: Get $15 of in-app purchases for this game.

Bitcasa: Bitcasa is another cloud storage service. Samsung offers 1 TB of free storage for three months.

Colassatron: Samsung offers this game for free (normally $.99) and some bonus content.

Asphalt 8: Samsung offers unlocked bonus content.

Fruit Ninja Android: Download this app for free and get extra content.

EasyDo Tablet: This app offers public transit alerts, trending Instagram photos, birthday tracking, and other services. Samsung offers a six-month trial subscription to add support and flight tracking.

LinkedIn: LinkedIn offers a three-month Premium subscription.

PayPal: The Samsung PayPal app can use the fingerprint reader on the Galaxy Tab, but Samsung is also throwing in $50 in coupons to select merchants when you pay using PayPal.

NYTimes Breaking News: Get a 12-week trial subscription and stop hitting your 10-article limit every month.

M-Go Movies + TV: This is a movie and TV rental and purchasing app. Samsung is offering a $13 coupon for services.

Hunger Games

The Samsung Galaxy Tab also comes with a limited promotion for a free download of *The Hunger Games* and *Catching Fire*. You download these movies by first downloading the Hunger Games app from Google Play and then using it to download the movies. The app will detect that you have the proper device.

Half-Price Case

As of this writing, Samsung offered a bonus purchase of an accessory such as a case (including ones with a built-in keyboard) for half price. Before you go too crazy, here are a few things to keep in mind.

The keyboard cases are often out of stock or backordered, and they're probably listed as double the price that Samsung wants to charge, anyway. Rather than anchoring yourself at a much higher price (currently $149 for a matching bronze keyboard case, so $75 with the discount), think of half price as the FULL price for that accessory and then do some comparison shopping from third-party vendors. A quick search on Amazon showed a number of $30 keyboard cases for the Galaxy Tab S 10.5. If you take your tablet with you to an electronics store such as Best Buy, you can probably find exactly what you need for less than Samsung's full price.

To redeem your Samsung offer:

1.   Create a Samsung account (Chapter 1 goes over this).

2.   Register your Galaxy Tab S.

3.   Receive the offer by email.

Summary

In this chapter, we explored the main sources for free or discounted Samsung content, including sample magazines, movies, free apps, and discounts on accessories.

In the next chapter, we'll dive deeper into apps and learn about three easy places to download apps for your device.

Chapter **4**

Three Ways to Install Apps

In the last chapter, we looked at some of the bonus content you could download and purchase from owning a Samsung Galaxy Tab. In this chapter, we'll get to the heart of installing and buying apps. We'll look at not one, not two, but three ways to purchase and install apps with relative safety.

Android's Unwalled App Garden

You may have heard Apple iOS referred to as a "walled garden," because you can only purchase or install apps from the Apple App Store on your iPhone or iPad unless you take drastic measures to "jailbreak" or "root" the device and defeat the default limitation on your phone or tablet. There are some good reasons why Apple limits you to only the App Store. They test every app for safety before allowing it into the App Store, and they can pull apps from your device automatically that turn out to be unsafe (a hidden virus or security breach, for example). However, Apple's choices for app approval have been sometimes controversial. Some developers have accused Apple of being anticompetitive and arbitrary on approval of apps.

With Android, this is not a problem. It is an "unwalled garden." You can install apps from as many different app markets as you'd like (or no market at all). I still suggest sticking to the big players for safety reasons, which is why I'm going to show you how to install apps from three of them: Samsung, Google Play, and Amazon. These are all large markets with a decent reputation for safety, and two of them are already preinstalled on your device.

Galaxy Apps

You had the chance to register for a Samsung account when you initially set up your tablet (Chapter 1), and you had a chance to download some Samsung apps with your Samsung bonus content (Chapter 3).

You can get to the Samsung app market, Galaxy Apps, by clicking on the "Galaxy Essentials" widget on your Home screen, but if you have removed this widget, you can still get to the Galaxy App store.

First, tap on the app tray icon (Figure 4-1).

Figure 4-1. Tap on the apps icon

Next, tap on the menu/options (Figure 4-2).

Figure 4-2. *Menu/options*

Now select GALAXY Essentials from the menu (Figure 4-3).

Figure 4-3. *Select GALAXY Essentials*

You may recall this as the familiar screen from Chapter 3. This is a featured area that shows multiple apps. Tap on Samsung GALAXY Apps to see more apps available from Samsung's market (Figure 4-4).

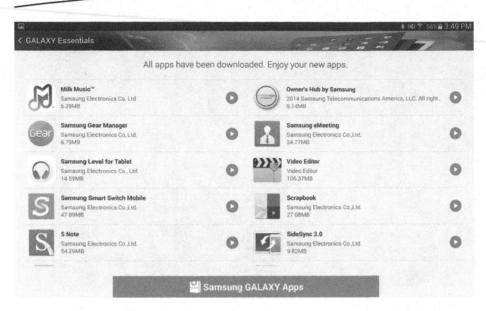

Figure 4-4. Tap on Samsung GALAXY Apps

In this area (Figure 4-5), you'll see featured apps, including staff picks, exclusives, and top downloads. You can also search for apps or find apps by category.

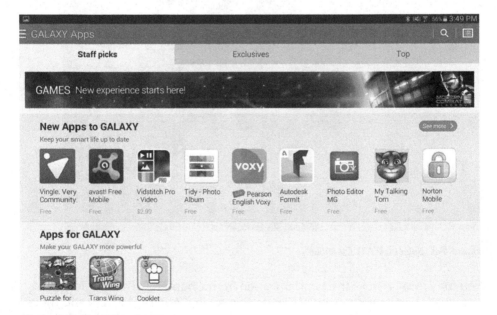

Figure 4-5. The Galaxy App store

Once you find an app that you like, you can tap on it to download. If you want to purchase an app, you'll need to make sure you have credit card information on file with Samsung. In this case, we'll download the free Autodesk FormIt app.

Tap on the app to see more information, including a summary of what it does, user ratings, and screen shots (Figure 4-6).

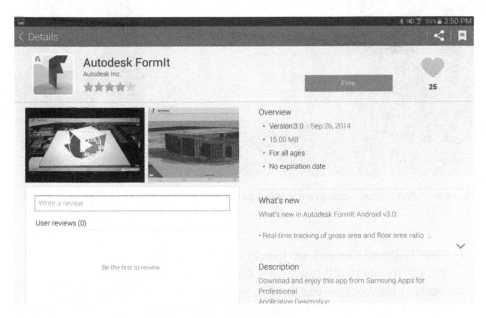

Figure 4-6. The details about the app on the Galaxy App store

If you want to download the app, tap on the "Free" button. If this app were a premium app, the button would say "Purchase" instead. Once you do this, you'll see a screen detailing exactly how much permission you're giving the app (Figure 4-7).

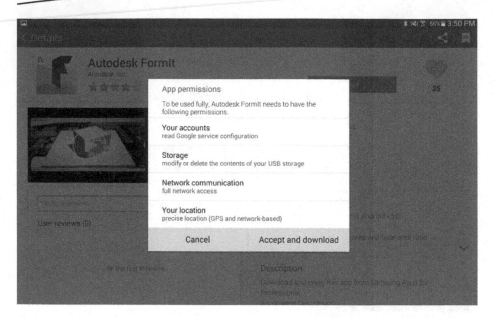

Figure 4-7. Permissions—either cancel or accept them and download

> **Note**   Although it's easy to get fatigued with all these permissions
> screens, it's important to read through them. If you have a game that
> wants permission to see your contacts, for example, ask yourself if that's a
> reasonable permission for that game, and do not download the app if the
> answer is "no."

Once you accept and download an app, you'll see a status message in the
notifications area, and you'll be able to open and use the app on your tablet
when the downloading is finished.

Google Play

The second area to download apps is really the primary area for most
Android users. The Google Play store was previously called the Android
Market, but now it contains all of the items that Google sells, including apps,
books, movies, and music. The online version even contains devices such
as tablets, watches, and phones.

You don't have to do anything special to install the Google Play store. It's already on your device. You do need to have an active Google Account, if you have not set one up already. You also need a credit card on file in order to purchase apps from Google Play.

Google Play App

To access Google Play, go to the app area, and tap on Play store, as shown in Figure 4-8.

Figure 4-8. Tap on Play Store

It may also be on one of your Home screens. It's installed there by default, but you may have added or removed the icon shortcut.

One you launch the Play Store app, you'll go into Google Play (Figure 4-9).

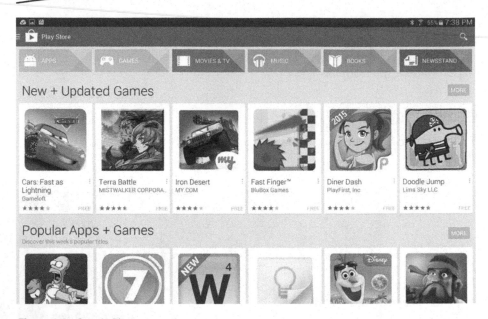

Figure 4-9. Google Play

You can see that this is more of a full-fledged app store. Indeed, it is the largest Android store and the primary store for most Android tablets. A few Android tablets, for example, the Kindle Fire, do not use Google Play at all and cannot use this store.

You can navigate by category tab, such as app or game. You can search for individual apps. You can browse by popularity or by editor's picks, and you can search for either premium or free apps. You can also buy or rent movies, eBooks, newspapers, and music from the same app and using the same payment system to download. Because the areas are color-coded, it should be less confusing to figure out if you are browsing for apps or movies (sometimes there's an app and a movie with the same name). Figure 4-10 shows the movie store as a point of comparison.

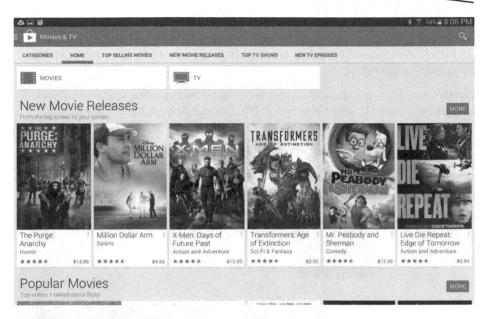

Figure 4-10. Google Play Movies and TV

If you enter the movie or book section by mistake, or if you ever want to find store options, tap on the left side of the screen as shown in Figure 4-11 and then tap Store home.

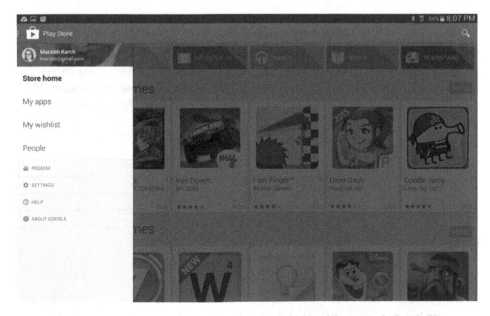

Figure 4-11. The menu you summon by tapping on the left side of the screen in Google Play

You can see the apps you've downloaded (from Google Play only—you won't see Samsung Galaxy App store downloads or other app stores here) and you can redeem gift cards or set your preferences to filter your choices by app maturity rating.

When you select an app, you'll see an area showing ratings, screen shots, and price, similar to what you see in the Galaxy App store (Figure 4-12).

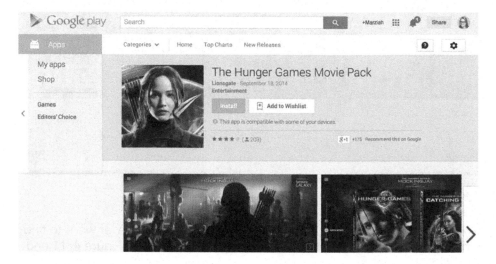

Figure 4-12. The app information page

If you want to download the app, tap on the Install button.

The app will show you all the permissions it requires, and it will also offer a drop-down menu to choose where to install the app. You may have more than one Android tablet or phone, or a combination of tablet and phone. You can actually select an app on one device and have it installed on a different device. Select your device and tap Install (Figure 4-13).

Figure 4-13. Install the app

You'll see a notification of download progress, and then you can use the app, just like the apps from the Galaxy App store.

From the Web

You don't actually have to use Google Play from your tablet or phone. You can also go to the website (play.google.com) when logged into your Google account (Figure 4-14).

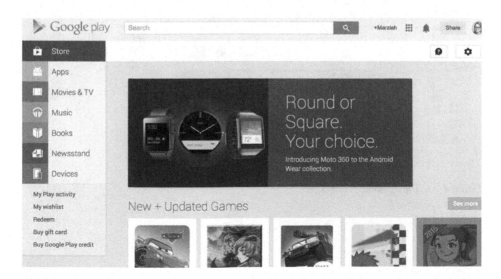

Figure 4-14. Google Play website

Remotely download apps or books from the website, and they'll download to your Samsung Galaxy Tab S and be waiting for you when you next use your tablet. You can use this same trick with most app stores, including Samsung and Amazon's. The option that you get from Google Play that you don't get from your tablet is the option to order devices. You can order a variety of hardware including phones, tablets, watches, Chromecasts, and Chromebooks, but you can't do this from the version of Google Play that runs on your tablet.

The Appstore for Android

The Amazon Appstore is the most complicated to install out of the apps we've explored so far, but Amazon offers a free paid app of the day, and sometimes they have specials with multiple apps, so if you're a persistent website visitor, you can establish quite the library of premium apps for free. You'll need an Amazon account to use the Appstore, which you should already have if you've ever purchased anything from Amazon.

First, visit the Appstore (www.amazon.com) from either your computer's browser or the browser on your tablet and go to the Appstore for Android (Figure 4-15).

Figure 4-15. The Appstore for Android

Now, click or tap on the Get Started area. This is going to walk you through the steps, but the important ingredients here are that you need to allow third-party apps, and you need the link to download Amazon's third party app. So, let's enable third party apps:

1. On your Galaxy Tab, tap on Settings (Figure 4-16)

Figure 4-16. Settings

2. Tap on Security

3. Tap on the checkbox next to "Unknown Sources." You'll see a dialog box asking you if you're sure you want to do this (Figure 4-17). That's because downloading apps outside the app store runs the risk that the app will have been maliciously written. Because we're going to use the Amazon Appstore, we're not entirely straying into apps from just anyone. Amazon tests their apps for compatibility and security, and by using the Amazon Appstore App, you allow Amazon to pull dangerous apps from your device—just like you do with the other two app stores.

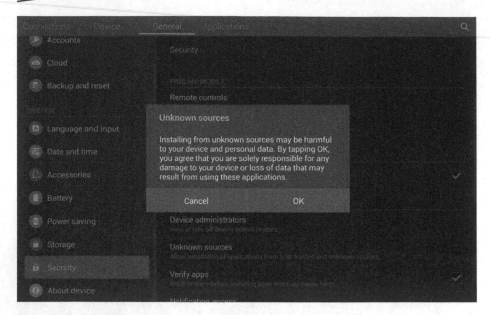

Figure 4-17. Confirm that you want to turn on this option

Now that you've taken care of the fiddly part with your Galaxy Tab preferences, you need to install the Appstore App.

You can get the app in one of several ways:

1. You can input your email on Amazon's Appstore page (Figure 4-18) or you can take a picture of the QR code with your tablet and follow the link. You also can type http://www.amazon.com/getappstore into your browser window or just tap on the link if you're looking at this page in your tablet's browser window.

Figure 4-18. Multiple ways to get the Appstore App

2.   Amazon will offer you a link to the app. Go ahead and tap on that. What you're going to download will be an .apk file. .apk is the extension that Android apps use, and if you hadn't enabled "unknown sources" in the preferences, Android just won't let you go any further.

3.   You'll see your downloaded .apk file in the notifications panel (Figure 4-19). Go ahead and tap on it.

Figure 4-19. Tap on the .apk file

4. You'll now see an alert showing you the permissions
    that the Appstore app requires (Figure 4-20), and
    you'll have the chance to Install or Cancel. Obviously,
    you want to Install.

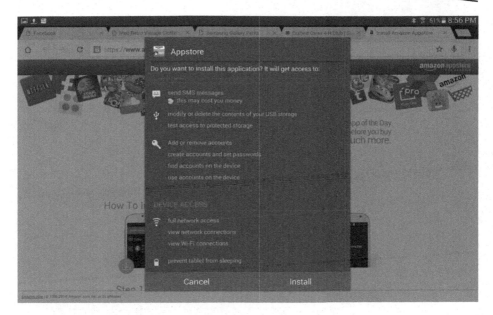

Figure 4-20. The Appstore app is finally being installed

5. Now you'll just need to click on the Appstore app when you want to download apps from Amazon.

6. Log in using your Amazon account.

The interface of the Amazon Appstore looks slightly different from the other app stores, but the basic information and concept is the same (Figure 4-21). Browse for apps and download them. The Appstore app can detect if you already have an app on your device from another app store, so you won't end up installing several duplicates of the same thing.

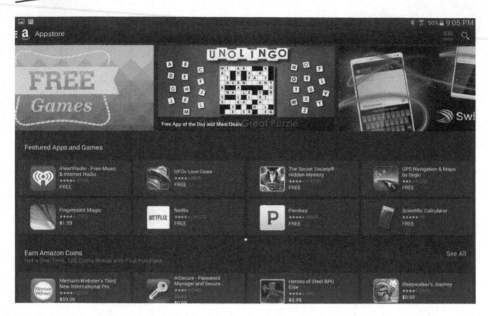

Figure 4-21. Amazon Appstore

If you purchase the "free app of the day" on Amazon on a regular basis (something I've done daily for years now whether or not I had a device that could even use them at times), you will amass quite the library of premium apps that you can install whenever you wish. Apps that you don't install will remain in your library for later use.

Other Third-Party Markets

Samsung and Amazon aren't the only app stores outside of Google. There's Getjar (http://www.getjar.mobi/) and countless other stores. Some may be more reputable than others. In general, I'd advise to stick with the three stores I've outlined in this chapter, because they come from large companies that vet the available apps.

Summary

In this chapter, we explored three different app stores. Two come automatically on your Samsung Galaxy Tab, and one (Amazon) is something that you have to download and install separately. You can find countless apps and bargain shop for deals in these three app stores.

In the next chapter, we'll start digging into using your device for business and pleasure. We'll set up a calendar, check email, look at Web conferencing, and go through other regular tasks.

Chapter 5

Business and Pleasure

We've spent the last several chapters setting up your tablet and downloading all the goodies. In the last chapter we looked at ways to install apps. In this chapter, we'll start looking at ways to use your tablet for business and pleasure. We'll also look at ways to set up security and share your tablet with the kids.

Let's get started by gussying up your Home screen. As you remember from Chapter 2, you have two alternative, widgetized layouts for your Home screen. There are six basic areas that can be populated by widgets that are useful to you. Let's start with the calendar.

The Calendar

By default, the calendar syncs to your Google Calendar, but it may also sync with other calendar apps at the same time (as long as they hook into the default calendar functions on your Android tablet). That means you're simultaneously displaying Google Calendar, "My Calendar," your Samsung calendar, and possibly some shared calendars from Google. Figure 5-1 shows the calendar.

Figure 5-1. Calendar widget

When you first try to add an event, you'll see an alert warning you that only "My Calendar" syncs with Samsung Kies. Samsung Kies is a desktop calendar syncing app that can run on Windows or Mac. If you're not using it, don't worry about this warning, and check the box saying that you don't want to see it again.

The calendar widget is in month view on one side, and events are only displayed for the day that you have selected. By default, the current day is shown so that you can keep track of your schedule. Add an event by tapping on the plus sign.

Choose which calendar to use. If you want this event to be visible on your Google calendar for other events, select that option (Figure 5-2).

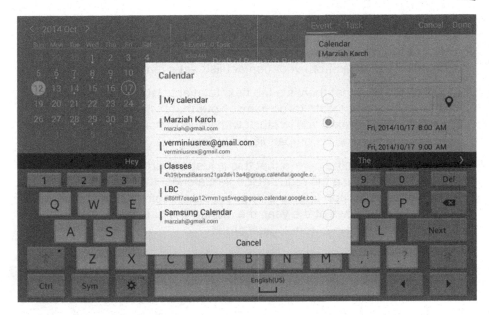

Figure 5-2. Select a calendar

Once you have selected a calendar, you'll have a wide variety of choices to make about the event (Figure 5-3).

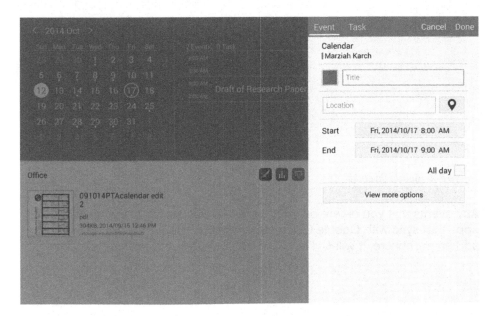

Figure 5-3. Choose your options

Give your event a title. You can choose a location either by entering a name or address or using the maps icon to select a location on a map. You can specify a start and stop date or designate it to be an all-day event. You can choose other attendees from your contact list, set a reminder, and more.

You may also notice that there's a tab next to events labeled "Task." If you tap on tasks, you can create to-do items. Note that tasks do not sync with Google Calendar. Instead, you're stuck with your Samsung calendar or any apps you've installed with compatible calendars.

The thing to keep in mind here is that this is just a shortcut widget. If it is not working out for you, use the regular Google Calendar (or other app) instead. The Google Calendar app (Figure 5-4) offers many more options for viewing your calendar with views of the year, the month, the date, and "Agenda," which just lists events in chronological order.

Figure 5-4. Google Calendar

Any events that you create on your Google Calendar will show up in any apps that sync with Google Calendar no matter where they are, so if you add an event here, it will still show up on your widget.

The Email Widget

The Email Widget (see Figure 5-5) uses your non-Gmail email addresses, including POP, IMAP, and Exchange. That means you can check and reply to Exchange work emails right from this widget but not Gmail messages. Well, that's not entirely true. You can check Gmail messages through POP or IMAP, but this will result in having two different apps checking the same Gmail account instead of just syncing data through a single app.

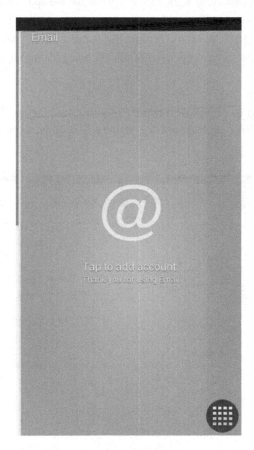

Figure 5-5. The Email widget uses the Email app, not Gmail

Note   If you sign up to check your Exchange email on your tablet, you may have to sign some very uncomfortable agreements about what your workplace is authorized to do to your device, including erase it. If you don't want to turn your device into a "company tablet," you can get an app that segregates Exchange data from the rest of the tablet functions (this means that the email widget won't work with it, either.) This way, if something happens, your workplace will erase just the app, not your whole tablet. My current favorite Exchange syncing app is Nine, which retails for around $10. You can use a free trial to make sure that it will sync with your Exchange account before downloading the full version.

Use the Gmail app to check and reply to Gmail messages, just as you'd use Google Calendar for calendar entries. Figure 5-6 shows the Gmail app in action.

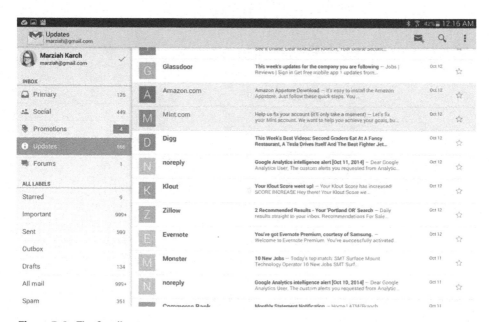

Figure 5-6. The Gmail app

Gmail is organized into multiple subinboxes. There's the primary inbox, for items that Google determines have been sent to you as an individual and therefore important.

> **Note**   Google is experimenting with a next generation email app called Inbox that integrates email, notes, and calendar items. If you'd like to try it out, you'll currently need to ask someone who is already using the service for an invite.

The Office widget includes a list of recently downloaded documents that you may edit or view by tapping.

The Quick Briefing widget includes space for Bing or Yahoo bookmarks, items for the day, and stocks.

Setting Alarms

To set alarms, use the Clock app, as shown in Figure 5-7.

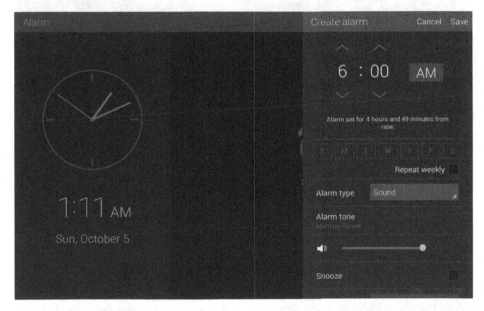

Figure 5-7. The clock app

Tap on the plus icon and you can add a new alarm. The Clock app allows you to set the alarm for the next day or a specific day or days of the week. You can check the box next to repeat weekly to set your standard work week alarm schedule, for example.

You can specify whether or not you'll include the snooze button as an option.

If you scroll down a little further, you'll see that you have the option to set a "smart alarm" (Figure 5-8).

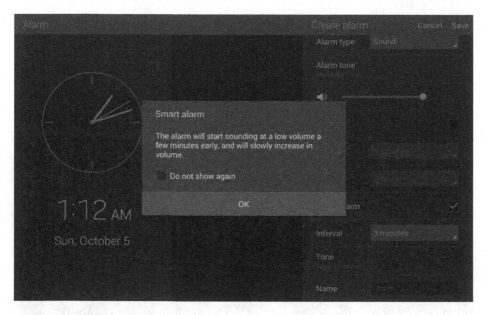

Figure 5-8. A smart alarm

Smart alarms can be set with or without snooze.

Creating Device Security

The Samsung Galaxy Tab allows you to set several methods for locking your tablet. You can have no security at all, which is fine if you live by yourself, don't have any personal or credit card information associated with your device, and will never ever let it out of your sight. For the rest of us, security is in order.

Go to Settings: Device: Lock Screen to set your lock screen security. The default level is Swipe, which means no security. You unlock the device by swiping anywhere. You can change to pattern, PIN, password, or—my favorite—fingerprint swipe. The first time you select this, you will need to set up your fingerprint by swiping your finger on the screen until it is calibrated (Figure 5-9).

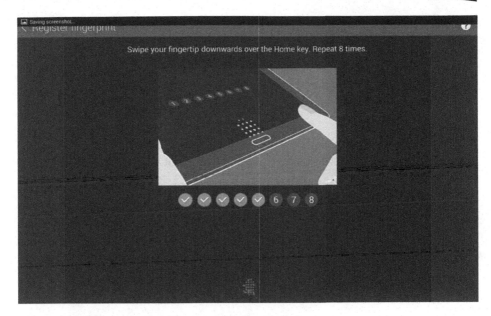

Figure 5-9. Keep swiping until your fingerprint is calibrated

When you use fingerprint unlocking, you swipe your finger on the bottom of the screen. This works fairly well most of the time, but if you mess up too many attempts to unlock your screen, it will make you wait 30 seconds before trying again.

Adding Family Members

In Settings, select users to add more than one user for your account. This creates new profiles that won't share data (so you don't mix up each other's emails or game high scores). If the account is for a child, set up a "Limited account." Limited accounts allow you to specify exactly which apps the account can use. This way, a child can play games but not use Dropbox or email, for example.

Siri-ish

Samsungs don't come with Siri. That's for iPads. You do, however, get two choices for Siri-like functions using voice commands. The first option, S-Voice, can be invoked by double-pressing on the center physical button on the bottom of your tablet. Try offering commands like "weather." You just say the word instead of asking a question.

The second option is Google Now. Use the Google search widget and tap on the microphone. If you are already in a search, you don't need to tap on the microphone. You can just say, "OK, Google." Google Now uses natural phrases, so ask "What's the weather?" and see the answer that you receive. The quality of the voice is much better for Google Now as well.

Summary

In this chapter, we explored using the tablet for work and home use.

In the next chapter, we'll look at viewing books, movies, newspapers, and more, and we'll show you how you can connect to other devices to get the most out of your tablet.

Chapter 6

The Galaxy and the Rest of the Universe

In the last chapter, we looked at using your Tab for fun and for business. In this chapter, it's all about the accessories. Let's look at using a Tab with Bluetooth devices, watches, phones, TVs, and more.

The Universe of Bluetooth

Bluetooth is a short-range wire replacement technology. With Bluetooth, you can do many things that would otherwise have required that you plug something in, such as connecting devices to keyboards, mice, headphones, and printers. You can also use Bluetooth to transfer files between devices without using a USB cable or Wi-Fi connection. Thanks to improved Bluetooth technology, you can even listen to your music in stereo.

The name *Bluetooth* came from a Danish Viking credited with uniting Scandinavians, King Harald Blåtand. His name is roughly translated as "blue tooth." The idea is that just as King Blåtand united Denmark, Bluetooth technology unites all your devices.

There are a lot of technical terms associated with Bluetooth technology, but it's not my intent to bog you down with jargon. We'll explore extending your tablet with Bluetooth and using devices such as keyboards and headphones or transferring files to your laptop.

> **Note** You must have a compatible Bluetooth adapter or device in order
> to stream music or use keyboards on your tablet. Not all devices are
> compatible with each other.

Turn on Bluetooth

If you're going to use Bluetooth on your device, you need to make sure that
it's active:

1. Tap on Settings

2. Tap on the Connections tab (if not already selected)

3. Tap on Bluetooth

4. Move the slider from off to on

Figure 6-1 shows Bluetooth enabled.

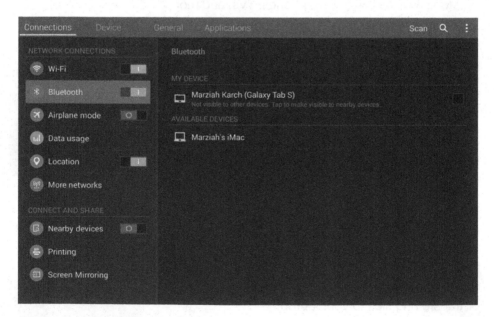

Figure 6-1. Active Bluetooth waiting to find devices

If you want to pair your device with computers or phones, you'll also need to check the box next to the Galaxy Tab S in the list to allow other devices to see it. By default, it is only visible to paired devices. This is for security. Once you've paired your Tab with your phone or computer, you can set the visibility to paired devices only.

Bluetooth Profiles

Bluetooth profiles determine how devices interact with each other and control things such as printing, transferring files, playing sounds, and using devices such as joysticks. In order to be compatible, both items have to understand the same profile. That means that you'll have to check with your tablet and your device to make sure that they're compatible. As a rule of thumb, they usually are.

The Galaxy Tab S supports:

- *A2DP (Advanced Audio Distribution Profile)—used for streaming audio to headphones*

- *AVRCP (Audio Video Remote Control Profile) —used for remote controls for your tablet*

- *DUN (Dial-Up Network)—used for tethering and modems*

- *FTP (File Transfer Protocol) —a method for transferring files*

- *OPP (Object Push Profile)—another method of transferring files from one device to another*

- *PBAP (Phone Book Access Profile) —used to access or transfer your contact list*

Bluetooth and Pairing

Bluetooth can communicate with other devices up to 30 feet away, but it has to know which device to communicate with. You can't just have random devices controlling each other and sending data. The process of connecting two Bluetooth devices with each other is called *pairing*. Not all devices are compatible with each other, so not all devices can be paired.

Pairing with phones uses the same process, but there's one key detail that you don't want to forget: both devices need to be discoverable. Both your tablet and your phone are generally not discoverable by default, so you'll want to make both devices discoverable (see Figure 6.1).

Pairing with Keyboards and Headsets

Accessories such as keyboards and headphones are easy to pair because they use a simplified system. Let's walk through pairing a simple, portable speaker.

Go into your Bluetooth settings (Figure 6.1). Most Bluetooth headphones, keyboards, and speakers have some sort of button to press or hold down that will cause the accessory to go into discovery mode. Press it, and then tap "Scan" to find a list of available devices (Figure 6-2).

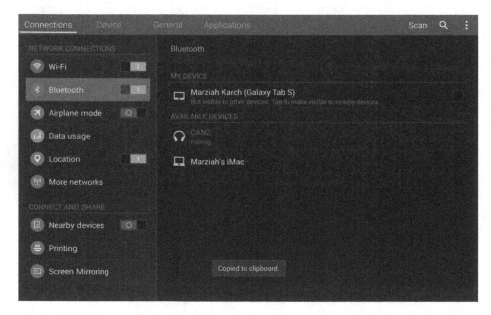

Figure 6-2. Scan for devices

Notice how the two devices that Bluetooth found have two different symbols. Tap on the CANZ device to pair it. The pairing is already in process in Figure 6-2.

Once it is paired, you'll see a "settings" icon next to the device, along with a message that it is connected (Figure 6-3).

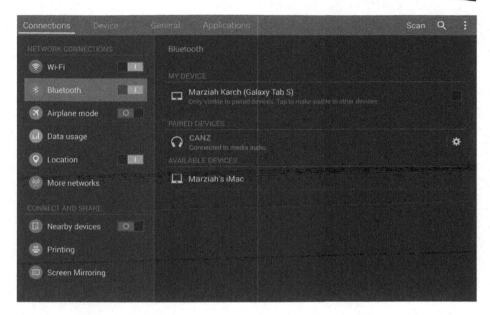

Figure 6-3. The speaker is paired

The settings allow you to specify that you want the speaker to play all media (meaning all the movies and music) or unpair the device.

Once you're paired, the tablet will assume that you want to use the paired device whenever it is in proximity. You won't need to repair the devices unless one device is somehow reset to factory defaults.

Pairing Phones and Computers

Computers and phones require a slightly more complicated two-step pairing, in which you must confirm the pairing on both devices. On older computers and some devices (including the LEGO EV3), you may have to type a number into the tablet and computer (Figure 6-4).

Figure 6-4. Pairing when numbers are required

However, on many newer computers and phones, you just have to confirm that a number matches on both your tablet and the device. The process is the same on a computer as it is on a phone. Figure 6-5 shows the simplified dialog.

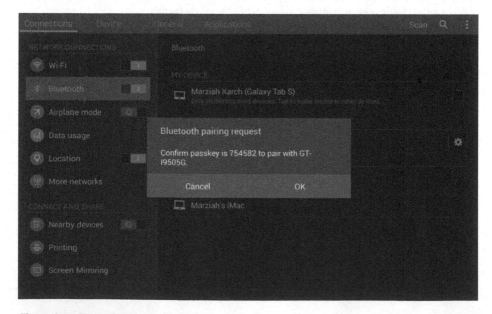

Figure 6-5. The simplified pairing dialog

Note   The reason that you have to confirm or enter a number on both devices is because there may be another device with a similar name on the network. This prevents confusion and adds a layer of security just in case.

Now, why would you want to pair your phone or your computer? Easy file transfer. Not to get too meta, but Figure 6-6 shows a Bluetooth transfer of images. The images, which you can see in the background, were actually the screen captures used to write this chapter. Rather than using a cable to connect the tablet to a computer or using a third-party service like Dropbox or Google Drive, I just transferred these files from the Galaxy Tab to my computer's hard drive.

1. Go to the Pictures app

2. Select a picture

3. Press the options button (the three dots on the upper right corner of the screen)

4. Choose Share by Bluetooth

5. Choose a device

Figure 6-6. Using Bluetooth to transfer files

Using a Keyboard

Keyboards pair just like speakers. You find the button to enable Bluetooth discovery. You pair the keyboard.

You may want a keyboard if you're doing a lot of typing on office apps. You can essentially turn your tablet into a netbook in a pinch. I wouldn't say it's quite a desktop replacement, but 10-inch keyboards are surprisingly easy to use.

When your keyboard is off, the onscreen keyboard will appear as usual.

Remote Control

Remember that one of the supported Bluetooth profiles (AVRCP) is used for remote controlling other devices. Many keyboards offer options to play media and music, launch apps, start instant messaging, or browse the Web.

Your Samsung Galaxy Tab S also comes with a built-in TV remote for Samsung (and a few other brand) TVs. By using the WatchOn app that comes with your Galaxy Tab S, you can use your tablet as a TV guide, set yourself a reminder to watch your favorite show, and then use the TV remote control to tune the TV (Figure 6-7).

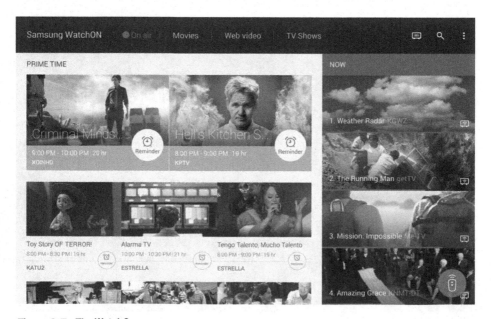

Figure 6-7. The WatchOn app

Tap on the remote button on the bottom right corner, and the app will take you through the process of setting up your remote (Figure 6-8).

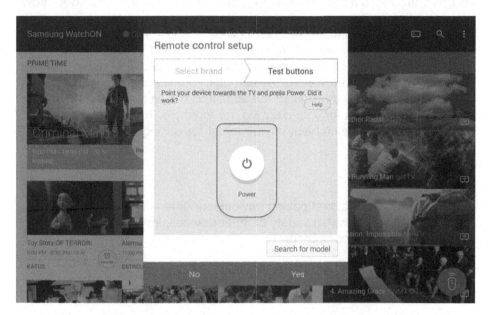

Figure 6-8. The remote is being set up

This is not Bluetooth pairing. The Samsung Galaxy Tab S actually comes with an infrared blaster that signals to the TV. Different TV models have different codes, so the app figures out the codes that will work with the individual device.

Roku

If you have a Roku, you can download the Roku app to control it, but you can also transfer pictures to the Roku using network sharing.

Chromecast

Google introduced this $35 streaming wonder, and it's actually pretty wonderful. If you purchase or rent Google Play movies (such as the free Hunger Games movies that come as a limited time promotion with the Galaxy Tab S), you can simply hit the "cast" button and send the movie to your TV. This also works with music.

Samsung Gear

Android introduced a new version of Android just for watches, called Android Wear. Previously, Samsung had a version that only ran on Samsung devices. The latest Samsung watch—the Samsung Gear Live—uses the latest Android Wear protocol. If you have a compatible Android smart watch—either one of the Samsung Gear watches or an Android Wear watch—you can use the Gear app to control your watch. You can pair your watch and tablet (this is a Bluetooth pairing) and then select the apps and media that you want to add to it. Add some songs for your daily jog, for example. Transfer photos that you took from your watch back to your tablet for editing.

Summary

In this chapter, we explored pairing devices and interacting with hardware. Use your Galaxy Tab with a variety of other devices, from keyboards and speakers to TVs and computers.

Index

Get the eBook for only $10!

Now you can take the weightless companion with you anywhere, anytime. Your purchase of this book entitles you to 3 electronic versions for only $10.

This Apress title will prove so indispensible that you'll want to carry it with you everywhere, which is why we are offering the eBook in 3 formats for only $10 if you have already purchased the print book.

Convenient and fully searchable, the PDF version enables you to easily find and copy code—or perform examples by quickly toggling between instructions and   applications. The MOBI format is ideal for your Kindle, while the ePUB can be utilized on a variety of mobile devices.

Go to www.apress.com/promo/tendollars to purchase your companion eBook.